LEARN TO CROCHET
FOR BEGINNERS

crochet *now*

First published in 2024 by Practical Publishing International Ltd.

Text and image copyright © 2024 Practical Publishing International Ltd.

ISBN: 9798328410007

www.practicalpublishing.co.uk

All rights reserved.

CONTENTS

STITCHES

PROJECTS

GETTING STARTED

Welcome to Learn to Crochet for Beginners, where we will take you through all the basics you need to get started with crochet

Brought to you by the experts at

crochet *now*

This craft is no longer just for the 'old fashioned' – crochet has really risen in popularity over the years and the things you can create with just a hook and a ball of yarn are limited only by your imagination!

Crochet is everywhere online and on the high street – and it doesn't look like it will be going anywhere anytime soon, so why not join the craft revolution and make your own fashion tops, accessories and even toys (also known as amigurumi)?

This guide is aimed at beginners who are just starting out on their crochet journey, and our expert step-by-step guides should give you the foundation you need to get started with following a pattern. We've included eight patterns for you to get your hook stuck into, from an easy one-ball chunky hat, to a beautiful baby blanket that you can gift to new arrivals.

Made by yourself   Peter Fehrentz

Amigurumi
The Japanese art of crocheting small, stuffed creatures that are cute or 'kawaii'

Hooks

The anatomy of a crochet hook

Head
This is the part of the hook that goes into your work when you make new stitches

Shaft
Also known as the shank, this is where your loops rest as you work and determines the sizes of your stitches. This is the important section when it comes to determining hook gauge and tension of your work

Throat
This section helps to catch and guide the yarn through your fabric as you work

Grip
Some hooks will have a groove for your thumb, making them more comfortable to hold

Handle
This is where you will mostly hold the hook, and can often have a soft or ergonomic design

To get started with crochet, all you really need are two things; a crochet hook and some yarn!

Crochet hooks come in all shapes and sizes, but they mostly look the same. The head, which is the part that goes in and out of your work and 'catches' the yarn to pull through, looks the same. The size of the hook is determined by the shaft, which is how large the hook is and therefore how large the stitches will be (for example 5mm).

Hooks can be wooden, bamboo, metal or plastic and can have a handle that is soft, polymer or ergonomic. As you crochet more, you will find a hook that you prefer to work with, which is especially important when you know how you prefer to hold your hook, which we talk a bit more about on page 10.

The size of the hook is designed to match the yarn you are using. Together, these create the desired tension of your work, which is the size of the stitches you need to make to ensure you match your pattern. Larger hooks will be used for chunkier yarns, and smaller hooks for thinner yarns.

Most beginners use a 4 or 5mm hook and a DK or aran-weight yarn – see the guide on page 6 for which hooks are recommended for which yarn.

Tapered

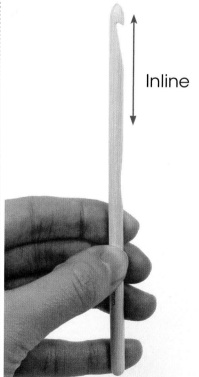

Inline

Some hook heads are inline (they match the handle width) and some are tapered (they are slightly larger). We recommend tapered heads for absolute beginners as it is slightly easier to hook the yarn with

US hook letter	UK hook number	Metric (mm)
-	14	2mm
B	13	2.25mm
-	12	2.5mm
C	-	2.75mm
-	11	3mm
D	10	3.25mm
E	9	3.5mm
F	-	3.75mm
G	8	4mm
-	7	4.5mm
H	6	5mm
I	5	5.5mm
J	4	6mm
K	3	6.5mm
-	2	7mm
L	0	8mm
M	00	9mm
N	000	10mm

Some patterns might use a different code to show which size hook they recommend, which you can match using this table

Tools

Yarn

After a crochet hook, your yarn is the most important tool in your collection when it comes to crocheting. It can feel like there is an overwhelming number of different types, materials, sizes and colours of yarn, but our guide should help you make a start.

4-ply
Recommended hook sizes: 2-3mm
Great for socks and summer accessories
Scheepjes Downton; 200m per 50g ball;
75% Merino 25% nylon

DK
Recommended hook sizes: 3-4mm
Great for toys and home décor
Yarnsmiths Create DK; 290m per 100g ball;
100% acrylic

USING A SMALLER HOOK FOR TOYS CREATES A STIFFER, MORE DENSE FABRIC

Aran
Recommended hook sizes: 4-5mm
Great for blankets and winter garments
Shown – Rico Essentials Vegan Cashmere;
100m per 50g; 100% polyamide

Chunky
Recommended hook sizes: 5-6mm
Great for winter accessories
Shown – Scheepjes Chunky Monkey;
116m per 100g ball; 100% acrylic

Super Chunky
Recommended hook sizes: 8-10mm
Great for quick makes
Shown – West Yorkshire Spinners Re:Treat
Super Chunky; 120m per 200g ball; 100% wool

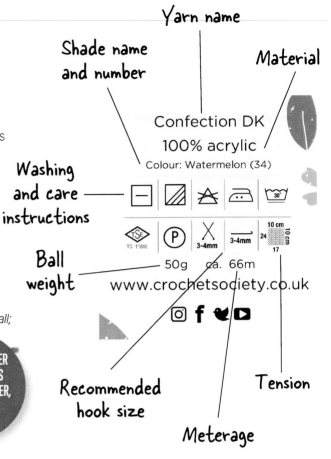

Yarn name

Shade name and number

Material

Confection DK
100% acrylic
Colour: Watermelon (34)

Washing and care instructions

Ball weight

www.crochetsociety.co.uk

Recommended hook size

Meterage

Tension

50g ca. 66m

Most patterns should tell you the weight of yarn you need, the recommended hook size and the amount of yarn needed.

The label on your yarn should give you all the information you need to get started, including material, meterage (length), colour name, weight and recommended hook size; if you don't see a crochet hook symbol don't worry, just match the knitting needle number. The label will tell you how to care for your yarn too (washing instructions) and the dye lot. This is especially important if you are making something that uses more than one ball in the same colour; the dye lot should match so that your colours also match.

We suggest beginners go up a hook size (by 0.5mm or 1mm) than the recommended size, to make it easier to see your stitches.

Other supplies

It's always handy to have a few other bits and pieces in your crochet tool kit to make sure you have everything you need to get hooking. All of these materials are readily available online or at your local craft shop.

Scissors
A small pair of sharp embroidery scissors or snips are a great, travel-sized addition to your kit and will ensure you are ready any time you want to change yarn or are finished with a project.

Darning needle
Use a darning needle to sew your finished pieces together, or to sew in any yarn ends after you have finished crocheting (to prevent any unravelling). Darning needles have large eyes, so you can thread the yarn easily, and can be plastic or metal.

Stitch markers
Stitch markers are invaluable when it comes to crochet! They can mark your beginning stitch when you are working in the round; they can be used to secure your work if you want to put it down for a while; and they can help with counting larger numbers on beginning chains.

Toy stuffing
Making super-cute toys? You'll need some super-soft toy stuffing to give them life and shape. Make sure you choose stuffing that is machine washable and safe for babies and children – check the product description for safety standards; look for compliance with EN71 in the UK and European Union.

Safety eyes
If you're making toys, you will need safety eyes to complete your characters; these are available in all shapes, sizes and colours, depending on what your pattern calls for.

Top tip
If you are starting a larger project and you need to chain a large number of stitches, use stitch markers as checkpoints at regular intervals so that you don't lose count

HOW TO GET STARTED

From holding the yarn to
working the basic stitches,
we will take you through the foundations
you need to become a crocheter

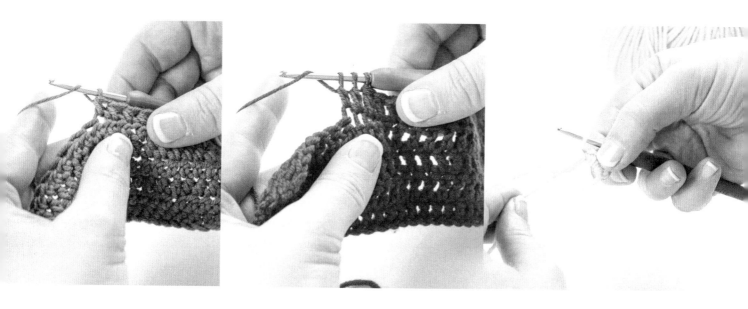

Guide to UK/US crochet terms	
UK	**US**
Double crochet (dc)	Single crochet (sc)
Half treble (htr)	Half double crochet (hdc)
Treble (tr)	Double crochet (dc)
Double treble (dtr)	Treble (tr)
Miss	Skip
Tension	Gauge

UK and US crochet terms are written slightly differently; we use UK terms in this book but if you want to follow a pattern in US terms you can use this guide to translate the pattern

Top tip
If you see single crochet (sc) in a pattern, that means it's written in US terms

HOLDING YOUR HOOK & YARN

Before you start crocheting, take some time to find a way of working that's comfortable for you

Holding the hook

PEN METHOD
There's no right or wrong way to hold your hook, but many crocheters find it comfortable to hold it as they would a pen, with your thumb around 4-6cm away from the tip of the hook and the hook facing down.

KNIFE METHOD
Others prefer the knife method, with the end of the hook resting against the palm of the hand for extra control of the hook, as you would a knife.

Top tip
Use your dominant or preferred writing hand to hold the hook. The step-by-step guides in this book are showing right-handed crochet, but holding a small mirror up to images will show how to work left-handed too!

Holding the yarn

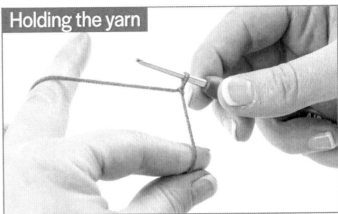

The key with crochet is to ensure even tension in the yarn. That means finding a comfortable way to hold yarn just taut enough so you can work with it. This technique shows the tail held between the index finger and thumb, and the working yarn over the middle finger.

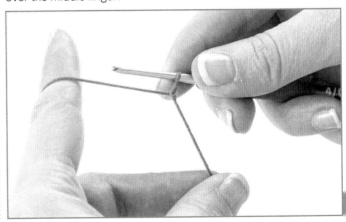

This technique shows the tail end held between the thumb and middle finger, with the working yarn wrapped around the index finger. Some people find it helpful to try loosely wrapping the working yarn over their little finger too!

Top tip
Finding a comfortable way to hold your hook and yarn will take time and practice, but the more you have a go the easier it will become!

MAKING A SLIPKNOT

Almost every crochet project starts with a slipknot, which connects your yarn and hook together for your very first stitch

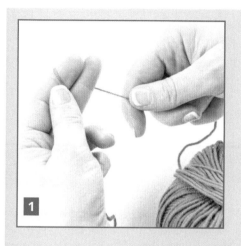

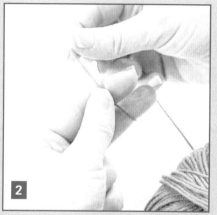

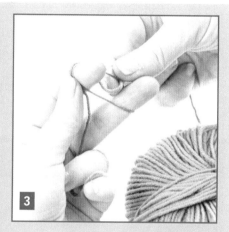

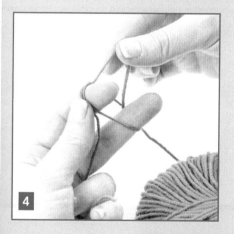

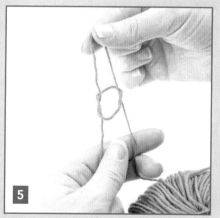

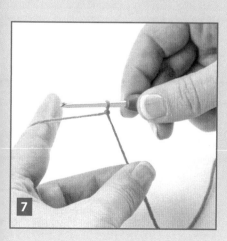

1 Holding the yarn end firmly, wrap the working end of the yarn over two fingers.

2 Cross the working end of the yarn over the top of the tail end at the top of your two fingers.

3 Spread your fingers apart to widen your loop.

4 Pull a loop from the working end of the yarn through the centre of the loop you've just made.

5 Remove the loop from your fingers and it should look like this.

6 Pull the tail end of the yarn to close the slipknot slightly.

7 Pop the slipknot onto your hook and pull tighter to close completely.

Top tip
Your slipknot should be tight enough to stay on your hook, but loose enough that it can smoothly move up and down the shaft

CHAIN STITCH (ch)

The chain stitch quite literally makes the foundation of all crochet patterns and stitches and is a great technique to practice to get more comfortable with your tension

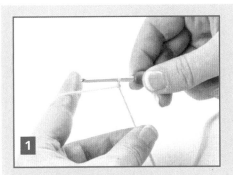

1 This is what the start of any crochet project looks like – a slipknot on a hook.

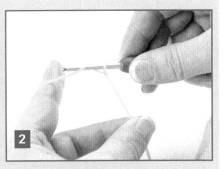

2 To begin making your first chain, first wrap the yarn around the hook (yrh) by bringing the yarn over the hook and towards you.

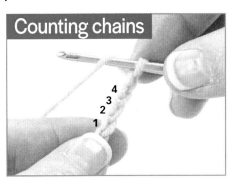

3 Pull the hook towards the first loop – being sure to move the hook rather than the yarn to make the stitch – and catch the yrh in the head of the hook.

4 Continue to move the hook until you pull your yrh through the first loop on the hook. You've now made your first chain stitch!

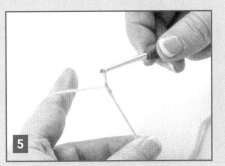

5 Your first chain stitches will likely be different sizes and tensions; this is fine!

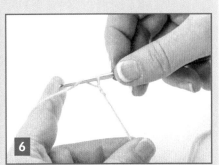

6 Keep working chain stitches by repeating steps 2-4 to practice.

Counting chains

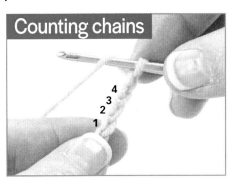

This is the top of your crochet chain – watch out for the little 'v' shapes which are the top of the stitches. To count how many chain stitches you have worked, you can count these little 'v's as shown; here you can see four stitches between the fingers.

Working into chain stitches

On the next page you will learn your next stitch, and the first to be worked 'into' your yarn (work) rather than just with your hook. This image shows how you should insert your hook into your work, which is under the 'v' shape that is the top of the crochet stitch. Let's give it a try!

Top tips

Always be sure to move the crochet hook and not the yarn when making your stitches

Gently pinch the chain stitch closest to the hook each time you work a stitch to keep a more comfortable grip on your work

DOUBLE CROCHET (dc)

A double crochet is an essential stitch in most crochet patterns, so once you've mastered it, you'll be well on your way to creating so many wonderful projects

1 Insert your hook into the next stitch from front to back.

2 Wrap the yarn around your hook.

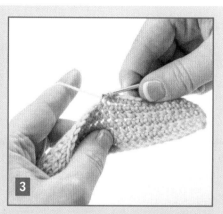

3 Pull up a loop through the stitch. You will now have two loops on your hook.

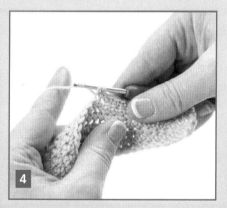

4 Yarn around the hook again.

5 Pull through both loops on the hook.

6 You've made your first double crochet!

Why not give these adorable amigurumi pals a try on page 32; they're made entirely from dc stitches

Top tip
Double crochet stitches (dc) are one of the first stitches you should tackle, as they form the basis of most projects from garments to toys and accessories. It may seem a little fiddly at first, but keep trying and you'll get the hang of it!

HALF TREBLE (htr)

Half trebles are medium-height stitches that appear slightly bigger and looser than a double crochet stitch; they're a great for blankets and cushions

1 Begin by wrapping the yarn around your hook.

2 Insert the hook into the next stitch, yarn round the hook again and pull through one loop. There will now be three loops on your hook.

3 Wrap the yarn around your hook again.

4 Pull through all three loops. That's one half treble complete!

Half treble crochet stitches are a staple in your stitch library!

Top tip
Half treble crochets are a smaller stitch, so they don't work up as fast. However, they can be really handy when working between small double crochets and bigger treble stitches

TREBLE CROCHET (tr)

Once you've learnt how to do a treble crochet,
you can pretty much complete
any crochet stitch!

1 The first step is to wrap the yarn around your hook.

2 Insert the hook into the next stitch and pull up one loop. There should now be three loops on your hook.

3 Wrap the yarn around the hook pull through two loops. There will now be two loops left on your hook.

4 Wrap the yarn around the hook again and pull through the remaining two loops. You've made a treble crochet!

This trendy tote on page 38 uses treble crochet stitches for a light and airy feel

Top tip
Treble crochet stitches create a more 'open' fabric. It's a great stitch to use if you want to add an airy feel to your designs, plus it works up quicker than a double crochet stitch!

DECREASING & INCREASING

Once you know how to increase or decrease, you can begin working on more complex projects that require shaping

Decreasing

Decreasing your stitch count requires a few more steps, but it's nothing that you haven't done before!

Double crochet 2 together (Dc2tog)

First, work a double crochet until you have two loops on your hook. Then, insert your hook into the next stitch along, yarn round your hook and pull up a loop. You should have three loops on your hook.

Wrap your yarn around the hook again.

Pull through all three loops on the hook. You've just double crocheted two stitches together!

Treble 2 together (Tr2tog)

Work a treble crochet stitch until you have two loops left on your hook.

Wrap the yarn around the hook again, insert it into the next stitch along and pull up a loop. There will be four loops on your hook.

Yarn around the hook again and pull through two loops on your hook. There should be three loops left on your hook.

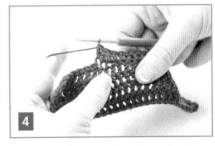

Yarn around the hook again and pull through all three remaining loops.

Increasing

You'll need to increase your stitch count quite often, especially when shaping garments or amigurumi. But don't worry, it's a super-simple technique and the same steps apply for all stitches.

Top tip
If you need to increase any stitch, be it a dc or a tr, just follow the same steps. Creating two stitches into the same place will give you an increase

To increase the number of double crochet stitches you have, simply make more than one dc into the same stitch. It's as simple as that!

SLIP STITCH & TURNING CHAINS

These two techniques will come up in almost
any crochet pattern you try your hand at,
so let's tackle them together

Slip stitch

These handy stitches are used to move along your work without
adding any extra height or increasing the stitch count.

To make a slip stitch, insert your hook into the next stitch in
the row.

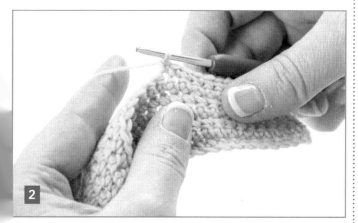

Wrap your yarn around the hook, pull up a loop and pull through
not only the stitch but also the loop on your hook.

Top tip
Slip stitches can be used for so many things, from joining
your work, seaming and even creating crochet edges on
your projects

Turning chains

Turning chains are used to raise your work up to the next level so
you can begin working the next row.

In this example, we're working a row of treble crochets. Begin by
chaining three at the end of the current row.

Turn your work and continue your treble crochet stitches along
the row. Remember, the beginning three chains do not count as
a stitch!

Top tip
Different stitches require a different number of turning chains
to match their height; double crochet stitches require one
turning chain before working into the next stitch, half trebles
require two chains and treble stitches require three chains

MAGIC RING

If you're looking to make some super-cute amigurumi toys, the magic ring will help you achieve a professional finish

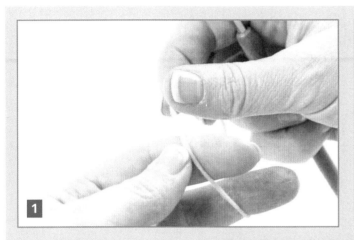

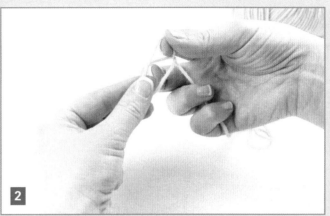

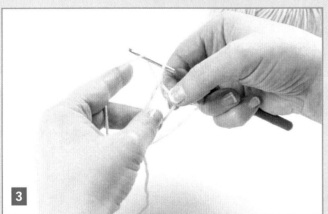

1 Begin by wrapping the working end of the yarn around your fingers to make a loop, similar to the start of creating a slipknot.

2 Pull through a loop of the working yarn and place your hook into the new loop. However, don't pull the tail to make a slipknot, instead hold the centre ring to stop it from moving.

3 At this point, the magic ring can be a little fragile, so to quickly secure it, make one chain stitch.

4 Continue to work the number of stitches required directly into the magic ring, ensuring both the loop and the tail end are caught in the stitches.

5 Pull the tail end of the yarn and the magic ring will close up. You've made your first magic ring!

Top tip
Magic rings allow you to have greater control over the size of the hole at the beginning of your projects, but remember that the ring will only tighten up as much as it can depending on your stitch count

WORKING AMIGURUMI STYLE

Once you've mastered your stitches, the next technique to learn is working in the round, or working in rows

Working in the round

There are two ways to start working in the round – one requires a magic ring and the other requires you to slip stitch a row of chains together to form a centre ring. In this example, we'll show you how to work using a magic ring.

1 Start by creating a magic ring and work the required number of stitches directly into the centre. Pull the ring tight to close.

2 It's important to place a stitch marker in the beginning stitch so you don't lose the start of the round!

3 Insert your hook into the first stitch, working into the top 'v' of the stitch, rather than the centre ring. Be sure to count your stitches at the end of each

round to make sure you're on track.
4 Continue working around the circle,

following your pattern and keeping track with your stitch marker.

Working in rows

Working in rows allows you to create flat projects that can then be seamed together if needed.

1 To start, you will need to create a foundation chain for you to work your first row of stitches into.

2 Often, patterns will include your turning chains in the original chain amount. In this example, we're working a row of trebles, so you would insert your hook into the fourth chain (skipping the three turning chains for a treble stitch).

3 Continue to work your stitches along the chain, until you have reached the end of your first row.
4 Once you reach the end, it's time to turn your work and move back the other way. Chain your three treble chains first.

5 Turning your work creates a right side (RS) and a wrong side (WS). The right side will be the one where the stitches look defined and appealing, but as you become more familiar with crochet, you'll be able to identify this easily.

LET'S MAKE A GRANNY SQUARE

Granny squares are iconic in the crochet world;
they're super versatile and easy to make
once you get the hang of them. Let's get started!

Hopefully you've mastered the basic stitches required to make a granny square, now you just need to put them together and begin your crochet journey. Follow our guide and you should be knocking out squares quickly and expertly in no time at all.

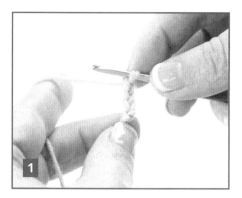

There are many ways to start a granny square, but a safe bet for the most simple of designs is to chain 4.

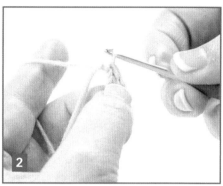

Next, work a slip stitch into the first chain to make a centre ring. This is the foundation ring you'll work your first round into.

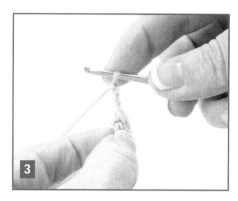

Once you've secured the ring, chain 3 more – this is called the turning chain (or t-ch), and is required to give you the height needed to make a double treble stitch. This turning chain will always count as your first treble stitch in this pattern – so be sure to count it as such.

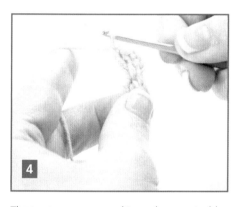

Then, you can proceed to make your treble stitches into the centre ring. We're using groups of three treble stitches together, so we've made an extra two, as the turning chain counts as our first treble stitch.

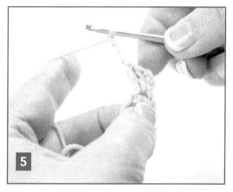

The corners of the squares are made by creating lengths of chains in between crochet groups. This pattern uses three chains in between each group, so make these now.

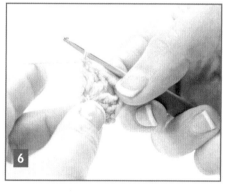

Then continue to work the next group of three treble stitches, again into the centre foundation ring.

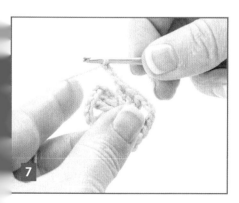

Continue as set until you have four groups of three treble stitches, then chain 3 for the next corner.

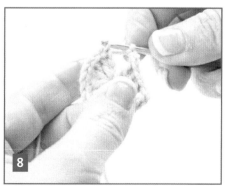

Insert the hook into 3rd chain of the beginning turning chain and secure with a slip stitch to join.

Your first round is complete!

Granny squares

One-colour squares

If you're only using one colour to make your granny square, there's no point fastening off the yarn after each round as that means more ends to weave in! However, we want to start each new round from a corner chain space, so here's what you do:

Slip-stitch into the beginning turning chain to secure the round.

Then continue to slip-stitch into the next two treble stitches consecutively.

Slip-stitch into the corner chain space and you've reached your destination.

Then, make the next beginning turning chain and you're ready to continue.

Multicoloured squares

If you're changing the colour in between rounds, you'll need to fasten off the current colour and add the new colour into a corner chain space.

Cut the working end of the yarn (that's the end leading to the ball), yarn around hook and pull through to secure the first round.

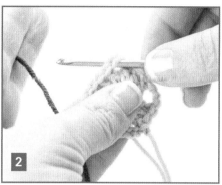

Pick up the next colour yarn and insert your hook into the corner chain space.

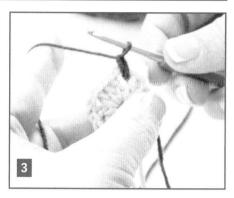

Yarn around hook and pull through the corner chain space to attach the yarn.

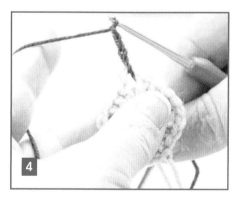

Make your turning chain in the new colour.

The next stitches are all worked into the corner chain spaces of round 1. Make a group of three stitches in the first corner (remember your turning chain counts as 1 treble stitch), chain 3 and then three more treble stitches in the same corner space.

Chain 1 in between corner chain spaces, and continue to work 3 trebles, 3 chains and 3 trebles into the next corner chain space. Repeat around and fasten off as before.

The next round is started in the corner as for round 2.

However, this time, you also work into the newly created 1-chain space. Make 1 chain before working into this chain space.

Make 3 trebles in this chain space – as this is not a corner space, you simply make the three trebles, chain one and continue into the next corner chain space.

Pompoms

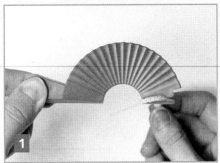

Attach your yarn to the notch at the front (semicircle edge) of the loom, with the working yarn behind the loom. Make sure to leave a few centimetres hanging over to tie your pompom together.

PERFECT POMPOMS

Use our simple how-to guide to make perfect pompoms all day long

Pompom makers, whether bought or made at home from cardboard, are usually a full circle shape. However, these looms are semicircle which makes them faster to cover with yarn. Take care to fill them as much as possible for lovely, plump pompoms.

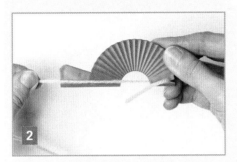

Carry the working yarn under the centre arch and bring from behind the loom to the front.

Hook the yarn into the notch at the back (handle edge) and take behind the loom.

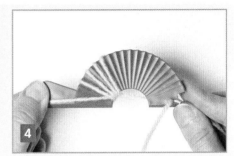

Working from front to back, wrap the yarn under the arch and over the top of the loom. Start at the edge closest to the handle and work to the opposite edge.

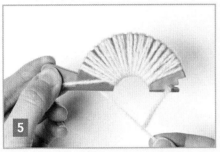

When you reach the opposite edge of the loom, continue wrapping but now in the other direction, towards the handle.

Repeat steps 4 and 5 until the loom is full. The more wraps you make, the fuller and more fluffy the pompom will be! If in doubt, wrap more times. Don't worry if you can't see the arch any more.

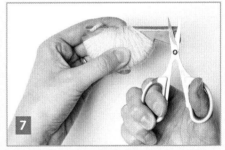

With sharp scissors, snip the loop that is hooked into the notch in the handle on the front of the loom.

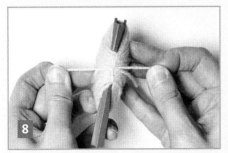

Gently pull the yarn (this should pull the yarn out of the opposite notch), being careful not to pull all the way through. Tie both ends of this yarn over your wrapped yarn, using a tight double knot.

Hold the loom with the handle away from you. The groove in the loom is at the front and allows you to insert scissors in the groove and cut the yarn. Cut the yarn all the way through, from this edge to the handle.

Remove the yarn from the loom and roll in your hand to fluff up. Trim to neaten.

SUPER SEAMING

Learn three must-know techniques for stitching your
project together – seaming clips at the ready!

Whipstitch

The invisible one: Great for garments, accessories, non-bulky seams
Drawbacks: Takes a lot of time, stitch matching is a must

Hold work RS tog, with tapestry needle and working front to back thread yarn under 2 sts together, pul.

Bring yarn back to front, thread under next 2 sts tog, pul.

Rep Step 2 to end, fasten off. Use a matching yarn colour to hide the seam.

Mattress stitch

The quick one: Great for blankets, cushions, toys
Drawbacks: Not as neat as other techniques

Hold work RS tog, with tapestry needle and working front to back, thread under the BLO of 2 sts tog, pul.

Work the same in next st, but working from back to front. Rep steps 1 and 2 to end, working loosely, then pull the thread gently to 'fuse' the edges tog.

This seam should be invisible from the right side of your work.

Double crochet

Our favourite: Great for texture, blankets
Drawbacks: Bulky, uses a lot of yarn

Hold work WS tog, with crochet hook, hook under 2 sts tog. Yrh, pul, 1 ch to secure.

Hook from front to back under next 2 sts, yrh, pul, yrh, pul (dc through both layers). Rep to end, fasten off.

You will finish with a clear row of dc on the right side of your work.

HOW TO READ A PATTERN

Now you know your stitches, it's time to put it all together and follow a crochet pattern!!

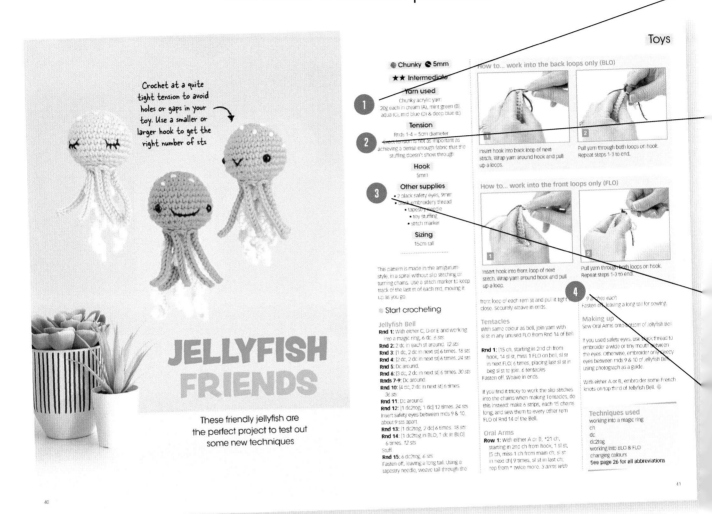

Crochet at a quite tight tension to avoid holes or gaps in your toy. Use a smaller or larger hook to get the right number of sts

JELLYFISH FRIENDS

These friendly jellyfish are the perfect project to test out some new techniques

Reading a pattern line

There are many different ways to write a crochet pattern, but all of our patterns use the same style, which we'll clarify here for easy reference.

Using numbered Rows or Rounds (Rnds) is the best way to keep your place in a pattern. Take notice of whether the pattern says Rows or Rnds, as it'll also signify whether you should be working the piece flat or in the round if not stated already.

The instructions for working a basic stitch will be given along with the instruction of how many stitches are worked in succession. For example, the instruction '4 dc' will tell you to work a double crochet stitch into the next four available stitches on the row below.

Increases are signified by the instruction 'in the same st' or 'in the next st'. As an example, '4 dc in the next st' will mean working four double crochet stitches into the

next available st.

Square brackets are used in patterns to show a complete instruction, which is then followed by a further instruction outside the bracket. For example, '[3 dc, 2 dc in the next st] 4 times' means that '3 dc, 2 dc in the next st' will be worked four times in succession.

Another way of indicating a repeat is to use *, followed by an instruction to repeat from a certain number of times.

Round brackets within pattern instructions will signify sizing – so make sure you pay attention to the Sizing section of the project materials column. If a pattern states S (M, L) then in the instructions 20 (24, 28) dc, you work the number of stitches required that corresponds to the size you are working only.

❶ Yarn

Using the correct yarn is really important! Making sure you have the correct yarn weight (such as DK or aran) and the correct amount will ensure that whatever yarn you use will be a great match for your project. If this doesn't match, your finished product could turn out a little different to what you were expecting.

❷ Tension

For most crochet projects, finding the correct tension is essential, especially for wearable items like garments, accessories and baby clothes. For example, you may be a really loose crocheter and if you don't match your tension your finished project may turn out the wrong size. If your tension isn't matching, try changing your hook size; move up a hook size if your square is too small, and down a hook size if it is too big.

❸ Other supplies

Before you get started on your project, it's a good idea to check you have all the extra bits you'll need such as stitch markers, toy stuffing and a tapestry needle. This way you can breeze through your whole project without any unexpected extra requirements.

❹ SBS images

If the pattern calls for it, we've included handy step-by-step images to help you combat those trickier parts of the pattern.

ABBREVIATIONS TABLE

beg	beginning
BLO	work in back loops only
CC	contrasting colour
ch	chain
ch-sp	chain space
cont	continue
dc	double crochet
dc2tog	work two double crochet stitches together
dec	decrease
FLO	work in front loops only
foll	following
inc	increase
MC	main colour
patt	pattern
pul	pull up a loop
rem	remaining
rep	repeat
rnd	round
RS	right side
sl st	slip stitch
sp	space
st(s)	stitch(es)
tr	treble crochet
tr2tog	work two treble crochet stitches together
WS	wrong side

Every pattern in this book uses the above abbreviations. If a pattern you are following has extra, it will often be included as a 'Special Abbreviation' with instructions on how to make the stitch.

INTO THE BLUE HAT

This super-simple hat will be ready for you to wear in just a few hours!

🧶 Chunky ⬤ 5 & 6mm

★ Beginner friendly

Yarn used
Chunky acrylic
100g in turquoise

Suggested tension
11 sts x 6 rows = 10cm
measured over tr

Hooks used
5mm
6mm

🧶 **Start crocheting...**

Rnd 1: Using larger hook, 4 ch, sl st to join.
Rnd 2: 12tr into ring. *12 sts*
Rnd 3: 2tr in each st around. *24 sts*
Rnd 4: [2tr, 1 tr in next st] 6 times. *36 sts*
Rnd 5: [2tr, 2 tr] 6 times. *48 sts*

Rnd 6: [2tr, 3 tr] 6 times. *60 sts*
Rnd 7: 1 tr in each st around to end.

Repeat Rnd 7 until work measures 19cm from beg when folded in half.

Ribbed Brim
Change to smaller hook.
Rnd 1: 4 ch, *turn, 4 dc in BLO, miss 1 st from last rnd worked, sl st, turn, 4 dc in BL, 1 ch; rep from * around edge of hat.
Fasten off. Weave in ends. 🧶

How to... work into back loop only (BLO)

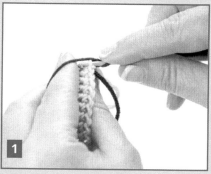

1 Insert hook into back loop of next stitch.

2 Wrap yarn around hook and pull up a loop.

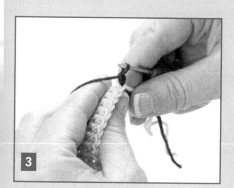

3 Pull yarn through both loops on hook.

4 Repeat steps 1-3 to end.

GRANNY SQUARE
CUSHION &
BLANKET

Create a cosy baby blanket or stylish cushion
cover with this classic technique

Techniques used
working into a magic ring
sl st
ch
dc
tr
changing colours
See page 26 for all abbreviations

🧶 DK 🌑 3mm

★ Beginner friendly

Yarn used

Acrylic DK
25g each in red (A),
light pink (B),
berry pink (C), cream (D),
deep blue (E),
light blue (F)
& yellow (G)

Tension

5 clusters x 10 rows =
10cm measured over patt

Hook used

3mm

Sizing

One size
Blanket: 50cm square
Cushion: Fits 30cm-square cushion pad

....

This pattern uses the classic Granny Square technique to create your choice of cosy homewares.

🧶 Start crocheting...

Work Granny Square pattern below, in the following stripe sequence: AA, BB, CC, D, EE, FF, GG, D, AA, BB, CC, D, EE, F, G.

Rnd 1: Working into a magic ring, 3 ch (counts as first tr here and throughout), 2 tr, [3 ch, 3 tr] 3 times, 3 ch, join with sl st to top of beg 3 ch. *12 sts*

Rnd 2: 1 sl st in each of next 2 tr, 1 sl st into 3ch-sp, 3 ch, [2 tr, 3 ch, 3 tr] into same 3ch-sp, *1 ch, [3 tr, 3 ch, 3 tr] into next 3ch-sp (corner); rep from * twice, 1 ch, join with sl st to top of beg 3 ch. *24 sts*

Rnd 3: Join yarn into any corner 3ch-sp, 3 ch, [2 tr, 3 ch, 3 tr] into same 3ch-sp, *1 ch, 3 tr in next 3ch-sp, 1 ch, [3 tr, 3 ch, 3 tr] into next 3ch-sp (corner); rep from * twice, 1 ch, 3 tr in next 3ch-sp, 1 ch, sl st in top of beg 3 ch.

Cont patt as set, working [3 tr, 3 ch, 3 tr, 1 ch] into each corner, *3 tr, 1 ch; rep from * to next corner 3ch-sp, along each side, changing colour as specified in stripe sequence.

CUSHION ONLY:
With D, work in dc to join edges as shown in photo. 🧶

AMIGURUMI
MINI PALS

These cute little characters perfectly
embody the spirit of amigurumi

Bunny

Dog

Mouse

Cat

Made by yourself   Peter Fehrentz

Techniques used
working into a magic ring
ch
dc
dc2tog
changing colours
working into BLO
See page 26 for all abbreviations

Don't be afraid
of colour changes,
they're easier than
they look!

🧶 DK 🪝 3mm

★ **Beginner friendly**

Yarn used

Acrylic DK
25g each in white (MC), blue (CC1), green (CC2), pink (CC3) & yellow (CC4)

Tension

29 sts x 36 rows = 10cm measured over dc

Hook used

3mm

Other supplies

- black embroidery floss
- toy stuffing
- stitch marker
- tapestry needle

Sizing

Each toy is approximately 9cm tall, excluding ears

....

🧶 Start crocheting...

This pattern is worked in the amigurumi style, in a spiral without slip stitching or turning chains. Use st marker or waste yarn to keep track of the first st of each rnd. Stuff your work as you go, making sure Head is stuffed firmly, and the bottom of each character is soft enough to stand flat.

Head & Body
Make 1 in each CC
Rnd 1: With MC and working into a magic ring, 6 dc. *6 sts*
Rnd 2: 2 dc in each st around. *12 sts*
Rnd 3: *1 dc, 2 dc in next st; rep from * to end. *18 sts*
Rnd 4: *1 dc, 2 dc in next st, 1 dc; rep from * to end. *24 sts*
Rnd 5: *3 dc, 2 dc in next st; rep from * to end. *30 sts*
Rnd 6: *2 dc, 2 dc in next st, 2 dc; rep from * to end. *36 sts*
Rnd 7: *5 dc, 2 dc in next st; rep from * to end. *42 sts*
Rnd 8: *3 dc, 2 dc in next st, 3 dc; rep from * to end. *48 sts*
Rnds 9-14: Dc around.
Rnd 15: *3 dc, 1 dc2tog, 3 dc; rep from *

to end. *42 sts*
Rnd 16: *5 dc, 1 dc2tog; rep from * to end. *36 sts*
Rnd 17: *2 dc, 1 dc2tog, 2 dc; rep from * to end. *30 sts*
Rnd 18: *3 dc, 1 dc2tog; rep from * to end. *24 sts*
Rnd 19: *1 dc, 1 dc2tog, 1 dc; rep from * to end. *18 sts*
Rnd 20: *1 dc, 1 dc2tog; rep from * to end. *12 sts*
Rnd 21: Dc around.
Rnd 22: *3 dc, 2 dc in next st; rep from * to end. *15 sts*
Rnd 23: *2 dc, 2 dc in next st, 2 dc; rep from * to end. *18 sts*
Rnd 24: *5 dc, 2 dc in next st; rep from * to end. *21 sts*
Rnd 25: With CC, *3 dc, 2 dc in next st, 3 dc; rep from * to end. *24 sts*
Rnd 26: *7 dc, 2 dc in next st; rep from * to end. *27 sts*
Rnd 27: *4 dc, 2 dc in next st, 4 dc; rep from * to end. *30 sts*
Rnd 28: *9 dc, 2 dc in next st; rep from * to end. *33 sts*
Rnd 29: *5 dc, 2 dc in next st, 5 dc; rep from * to end. *36 sts*
Rnd 30: *11 dc, 2 dc in next st; rep from * to end. *39 sts*
Rnd 31: *6 dc, 2 dc in next st, 6 dc; rep from * to end. *42 sts*
Rnd 32: Dc around, fasten off CC.
Rnds 33-38: With MC, dc around.
Rnd 39: *5 dc in BLO, 1 dc2tog in BLO; rep from * to end. *36 sts*
Rnd 40: *2 dc, 1 dc2tog, 2 dc; rep from * to end. *30 sts*
Rnd 41: *3 dc, 1 dc2tog; rep from * to end. *24 sts*
Rnd 42: *1 dc, 1 dc2tog, 1 dc; rep from * to end. *18 sts*
Rnd 43: *1 dc, 1 dc2tog; rep from * to end. *12 sts*
Rnd 44: 6 dc2tog. *6 sts.*

Fasten off, leaving a long tail. Stuff Head and Body. With tapestry needle, run yarn tail through rem sts and pull tight to close the bottom of the Body.

Ears
Make 2 of each

FOR BUNNY
Rnd 1: With MC and working into a magic ring, 6 dc. *6 sts*
Rnd 2: *1 dc, 2 dc in next st; rep from * to end. *9 sts*

Rnd 3: *1 dc, 2 dc in next st, 1 dc; rep from * to end. *12 sts*
Rnd 4: *3 dc, 2 dc in next st; rep from * to end. *15 sts*
Rnds 5-6: Dc around.
Rnd 7: *2 dc, 2 dc in next st, 2 dc; rep from * to end. *18 sts*
Rnds 8-10: Dc around.
Rnd 11: *2 dc, 1 dc2tog, 2 dc; rep from * to end. *15 sts*
Rnds 12-13: Dc around.
Rnd 14: *3 dc, 1 dc2tog; rep from * to end. *12 sts*
Rnd 15: *1 dc, 1 dc2tog, 1 dc; rep from * to end. *9 sts*
Rnd 16: *1 dc, 1 dc2tog; rep from * to end. *6 sts*
Fasten off, leaving a long tail.

FOR CAT
Rnds 1-3: As for Bunny
Rnds 4-6: Dc around.
Fasten off, leaving a long tail.

FOR MOUSE
Rnds 1-4: As for Bunny.
Rnd 5: *2 dc, 2 dc in next st, 2 dc; rep from * to end. *18 sts*
Rnds 6-8: Dc around.
Rnd 9: *2 dc, 1 dc2tog, 2 dc; rep from * to end. *15 sts*
Rnd 10: *3 dc, 1 dc2tog; rep from * to end. *12 sts*
Fasten off, leaving a long tail.

FOR DOG
Rnd 1: With MC and working into a magic ring, 6 dc. *6 sts*
Rnd 2: 2 dc in each st around. *12 sts*
Rnd 3: *1 dc, 2 dc in next st; rep from * to end. *18 sts*
Rnds 4-5: Dc around.
Rnd 6: *2 dc, 1 dc2tog, 2 dc; rep from * to end. *15 sts*
Rnds 7-8: Dc around.
Rnd 9: *3 dc, 1 dc2tog; rep from * to end. *12 sts*
Rnds 10-11: Dc around.
Rnd 12: *1 dc, 1 dc2tog, 1 dc; rep from * to end. *9 sts*
Rnd 13: *1 dc, 1 dc2tog; rep from * to end. *6 sts*
Fasten off, leaving a long tail.

Finishing

Using tapestry needle, sew Ears and Tail to Head and Body. Embroider the eyes using embroidery floss, using photograph as a guide. Weave in ends. 🧶

Pastel Rainbow

Bright Rainbow

LITTLE RAINBOW DELIGHTS

Celebrate love of all kinds with these delightful quick-make wall-hangings

🧶 DK 🌀 3.5mm

★ Beginner friendly

Yarn used
Pastel Rainbow
100g each in light green (A),
light blue (B),
purple (C),
light pink (D),
light orange (E)
& yellow (F)

Bright Rainbow:
100g each in green (A),
blue (B),
purple (C),
pink (D),
orange (E)
& yellow (F)

Hook used
3.5mm

Other supplies
• tapestry needle
• scissors

Sizing
16cm wide x 8cm high
(without tassels)

🧶 Start crocheting...

Rainbow
With A, chain 5. Join to first ch to work in the rnd.
Rnd 1: 2 ch (counts as first st), 11 tr into centre of ring, join. Fasten off. *12 sts*
Join F to last st and chain 2 (does not count as st throughout).
Rnd 2: [2 tr in next st] 12 times. Fasten off. *24 sts*
Join B to last st and chain 2.
Rnd 3: [2 tr in next st, 1 tr] 12 times. Fasten off. *36 sts*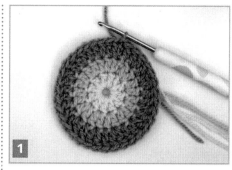

Techniques used
sl st
ch
dc
tr
changing colours
making tassels
See page 26 for all abbreviations

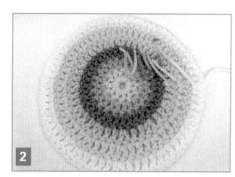

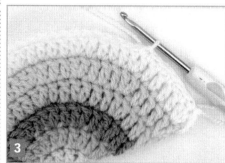

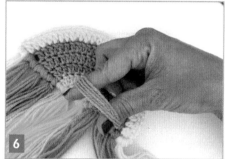

Join C to last st and chain 2.
Rnd 4: [2 tr in next st, 2 tr] 12 times. Fasten off. *48 sts*
Join D to last st and chain 2.
Rnd 5: [2 tr in next st, 3 tr] 12 times. Fasten off. *60 sts*
Join E to last st and chain 2.
Rnd 6: [2 tr in next st, 4 tr] 12 times. Do not fasten off. *72 sts*
Trim ends, but there is no need to weave in your ends as these will be enclosed in the next step.
Fold your circle in half, WS together, with beg st on RH side of semicircle.
Row 7: Working through both layers of

fabric, word 36 dc evenly across top of work, joining two edges together.
Fasten off and weave in ends.

Tassels
Cut five strands of yarn of each colour approximately 30cm long to match your rainbow stripes. Fold these in half and loop through the end of your stripes (base 2 tr). Loop yarn end through to make a Tassel and trim to even lengths.

Finishing
Tie a small loop at the top of your Rainbow to hang. 🧶

Techniques used
sl st
ch
tr
tr2tog
changing colours
making tassels
See page 26 for all abbreviations

RASPBERRY RIPPLE WRAP

This scrumptiously quick and easy accessory is light, airy and colourful – simply perfect to have around in the summer

🧶 Aran   ⬤ 5.5mm

★ Quick & easy

Yarn used

Cotton aran yarn
100g in light pink (A)
100g in cherry pink (B)
100g in pastel pink (C)
100g in bright pink (D)
50g in baby pink (E)
50g in soft pink (F)

Tension

11.5 sts x 6 rows = 10cm measured over tr

Hook used

5.5mm

Sizing

28x225cm

Check your stitch count regularly to ensure you have not dropped or added a stitch, as this will throw your ripple off.

Cotton yarn does not have as much stretch as acrylic or wool yarn, so make sure your tension is not overly tight while working with this yarn, or you will find it difficult to insert your hook into each stitch.

Beg 3 ch counts as first tr.

Join each new colour with a sl st in first st

after turning, fasten off previous colour.

🧶 Start crocheting...

With A, chain 259.

Row 1: Starting in 4th ch from hook (missed chs count as first tr), 6 tr, 2 tr2tog, 5 tr, *[2 tr in next st] twice, 5 tr, 2 tr2tog, 5 tr; rep from * to last st, 2 tr in last st. Turn. *256 sts*

Row 2: [3 ch, 1 tr] in first st, 5 tr, 2 tr2tog, 5 tr, *[2 tr in next st] twice, 5 tr, 2 tr2tog, 5 tr; rep from * to last st, 2 tr in last st. Turn.

Row 3: As Row 2.

Row 4: With B, as Row 2.

Rows 5-6: With C, as Row 2.

Rows 7-8: With D, as Row 2.

Rows 9-11: With E, as Row 2.

Row 12: With F, as Row 2.

Row 13: With A, as Row 2.

Rows 14-16: With C, as Row 2.

Rows 17-18. With B, as Row 2.

Fasten off. Weave in ends and block.

Fringe

Make 36: 6 in each colour.

*Cut 7 lengths of yarn each 40cm long, holding them tog, fold in half to form a loop. Insert hook between last and next st of row from back to front. Pull loop through to the back and thread the ends through loop; rep from * in each row across each short edge. Join in the following colour sequence: [A, B, C, D, E and F] 3 times on each side. Once they are all joined, trim to same length and steam to straighten if desired.🧶

Try using a yarn
with tweed-like
flecks in it for a
subtle pop of colour

Techniques used
sl st
ch
tr
tr2tog
working in joined rnds
sl st to join
working into ch-sp
See page 26 for all abbreviations

Magical Market BAG

This lightweight and stylish market bag is perfect for any trip to the shops

🧶 DK ⬤ 4mm

★ Beginner friendly

Yarn used

Cotton DK
200g in white or tweed-style white mix

Tension

20 sts x 8 rows = 10cm x 10cm
measured over tr

Hook used

4.5mm

Other supplies

• 2 locking st markers

Sizing

35cm deep x 30cm wide, strap: 50cm long

....

Beg 3 ch counts as first tr. Join each rnd with sl st in top of beg 3 ch unless otherwise stated.

🧶 Start crocheting...

With A, chain 48.
Rnd 1: Working into a magic ring, 3 ch, 11 tr, join. 12 sts
Rnd 2: [3 ch, 1 tr] in first st, [2 tr in next st] 11 times, join. *24 sts*
Rnd 3: 3 ch, 2 tr in next st, [1 tr, 2 tr in next st] 11 times, join. *36 sts*
Rnd 4: 3 ch, 1 tr, 2 tr in next st, [2 tr, 2 tr in next st] 11 times, join. *48 sts*
Rnd 5: 3 ch, 2 tr, 2 tr in next st, [3 tr, 2 tr in next st] 11 times, join. *60 sts*
Rnd 6: 3 ch, 3 tr, 2 tr in next st, [4 tr, 2 tr in next st] 11 times, join. *72 sts*
Rnd 7: 3 ch, 4 tr, 2 tr in next st, [5 tr, 2 tr in next st] 11 times, join. *84 sts*

Rnd 8: 3 ch, 5 tr, 2 tr in next st, [6 tr, 2 tr in next st] 11 times, join. *96 sts*
Rnd 9: 3 ch, 6 tr, 2 tr in next st, [7 tr, 2 tr in next st] 11 times, join. *108 sts*
Rnd 10: 3 ch, 7 tr, 2 tr in next st, [8 tr, 2 tr in next st] 11 times, join. *120 sts*
Rnd 11: 3 ch, 8 tr, 2 tr in next st, [9 tr, 2 tr in next st] 11 times, join. 132 sts
Rnd 12: 3 ch, 9 tr, 2 tr in next st, [10 tr, 2 tr in next st] 11 times, join. 144 sts
Rnd 13: 5 ch (counts as tr and 2 ch), miss next 2 sts, [1 tr, 2 ch, miss next 2 sts] 47 times, join with sl st in 3rd of beg 5 ch.
Rnds 14-18: 5 ch (counts as tr and 2 ch), miss first 2ch-sp, [1 tr, 2 ch, miss next 2ch-sp] 47 times, join with sl st to 3rd of beg 5 ch.
Rnd 19: 3 ch, 2 tr into first 2ch-sp, [1 tr, 2 tr into next 2ch-sp] 47 times, join.
Rnd 20: 3 ch, tr around, join.
Rnds 21-28: Rep rnds 13-20.
Rnds 29-35: Rep rnds 13-19.
Rnd 36: 3 ch, 9 tr, 1 tr2tog, [10 tr, 1 tr2tog] 11 times, join. *132 sts*
Rnd 37: 3 ch, 8 tr, 1 tr2tog, [9 tr, 1 tr2tog] 11 times, join. *120 sts*
Do not fasten off, continue to Strap.

Strap

Row 1: 3 ch, 11 tr, leave rem sts unworked. Turn. *11 sts*
Count next 48 missed sts along last rnd, place a marker in next st, count 9 more sts, place a marker in next st (9 sts in between markers).
Rows 2-40: 3 ch, 11 tr. Turn.

Begin joining Strap to opposite side with sl st through first st of Strap and first marked st on last rnd at the same time, [sl st through next st on Strap and next st on last rnd at the same time] 10 times, last join will be in 2nd marked st.
Fasten off. Weave in ends. 🧶

Crochet at a quite tight tension to avoid holes or gaps in your toy. Use a smaller or larger hook to get the right number of sts

JELLYFISH FRIENDS

These friendly jellyfish are the perfect project to test out some new techniques

● Chunky ● 5mm

★★ Intermediate

Yarn used

Chunky acrylic yarn
20g each in cream (A), mint green (B),
aqua (C), mid blue (D) & deep blue (E)

Tension

Rnds 1-4 = 5cm diameter
Exact tension is not as important as
achieving a dense enough fabric that the
stuffing doesn't show through

Hook

5mm

Other supplies

- 2 black safety eyes, 9mm
- black embroidery thread
- tapestry needle
- toy stuffing
- stitch marker

Sizing

15cm tall

This pattern is made in the amigurumi
style, in a spiral without slip stitching or
turning chains. Use a stitch marker to keep
track of the last st of each rnd, moving it
up as you go.

● Start crocheting

Jellyfish Bell

Rnd 1: With either C, D or E and working
   into a magic ring, 6 dc. *6 sts*
Rnd 2: 2 dc in each st around. *12 sts*
Rnd 3: [1 dc, 2 dc in next st] 6 times. *18 sts*
Rnd 4: [2 dc, 2 dc in next st] 6 times. *24 sts*
Rnd 5: Dc around.
Rnd 6: [3 dc, 2 dc in next st] 6 times. *30 sts*
Rnds 7-9: Dc around.
Rnd 10: [4 dc, 2 dc in next st] 6 times.
   36 sts
Rnd 11: Dc around.
Rnd 12: [1 dc2tog, 1 dc] 12 times. *24 sts*
Insert safety eyes between rnds 9 &
about 9 sts apart
Rnd 13: [1 dc2tog, 2 dc] 6 times. *18 sts*
Rnd 14: [1 dc2tog in BLO, 1 dc in BLO]
   6 times. *12 sts*
Stuff.
Rnd 15: 6 dc2tog. *6 sts*
Fasten off, leaving a long tail. Using a
tapestry needle, weave tail through the

How to... work into the back loops only (BLO)

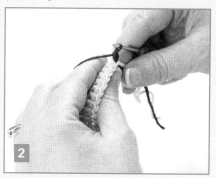

Insert hook into back loop of next
stitch. Wrap yarn around hook and pull
up a loops.

Pull yarn through both loops on hook.
Repeat steps 1-3 to end.

How to... work into the front loops only (FLO)

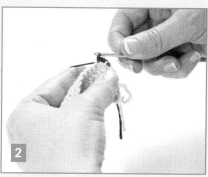

Insert hook into front loop of next
stitch. Wrap yarn around hook and pull
up a loop.

Pull yarn through both loops on hook.
Repeat steps 1-3 to end.

front loop of each rem st and pull it tight to
close. Securely weave in ends.

Tentacles

With same colour as bell, join yarn with
sl st in any unused FLO from Rnd 14 of Bell.

Rnd 1: [15 ch, starting in 2nd ch from
   hook, 14 sl st, miss 1 FLO on bell, sl st
   in next FLO] 6 times, placing last sl st in
   beg sl st to join. *6 tentacles*
Fasten off. Weave in ends.

If you find it tricky to work the slip stitches
into the chains when making Tentacles, do
this instead: make 6 strips, each 15 chains
long, and sew them to every other rem
FLO of Rnd 14 of the Bell.

Oral Arms

Row 1: With either A or B, *21 ch,
   starting in 2nd ch from hook, 1 sl st,
   [5 ch, miss 1 ch from main ch, sl st
   in next ch] 9 times, sl st in last ch;
   rep from * twice more. *3 arms with*

9 arches each
Fasten off, leaving a long tail for sewing.

Making up

Sew Oral Arms onto bottom of Jellyfish Bell.

If you used safety eyes, use black thread to
embroider a wide or tiny mouth between
the eyes. Otherwise, embroider only sleepy
eyes between rnds 9 & 10 of Jellyfish Bell,
using photograph as a guide.

With either A or B, embroider some French
knots on top third of Jellyfish Bell. ●

Techniques used

working into a magic ring
ch
dc
dc2tog
working into BLO & FLO
changing colours
See page 26 for all abbreviations

Sorbet Stripes
BLANKET

This timeless design will make the perfect gift for fans of pastel shades and ice cream

🧶 DK ⚫ 4mm

★ Try something new

Yarn used
Acrylic DK
400g in white (MC)
100g each in lilac (CC1),
yellow (CC2),
pink (CC3)
& mint (CC4)

Tension
24 sts x 24 rows = 10cm measured over
moss stitch (alternating dc and 1 ch)

Hook used
4mm

Sizing
112x84cm

Beg 1 ch counts as first dc unless otherwise stated. Make this chain fairly loose, to make it easier to work into.

Gently steam block before and after the border to make sure the edges are nice and neat.

Change colour on the last stitch of the previous row, completing the stitch in the new colour.

🧶 Start crocheting...

With MC, chain 240.
Row 1: 1 dc in 2nd ch from hook (missed ch counts as first dc), *1 ch, miss 1 ch, 1 dc; rep from * to end. Turn. *121 dc, 119 chs*
Row 2: 1 ch, 1 dc into first 1ch-sp, *1 ch, 1 dc into next 1ch-sp; rep to last 2 dc, 1 ch, miss 1 st, 1 dc in beg 1 ch. Turn.

Rows 3-14: As Row 2.
Change to CC1.
Rows 15-20: As Row 2.
Change to MC.
Rows 21-34: As Row 2.
Change to CC2.
Rows 35-40: As Row 2.
Change to MC.
Rows 41-54: As Row 2.
Change to CC3.
Rows 55-60: As Row 2.
Change to MC.
Rows 61-74: As Row 2.
Change to CC4.
Rows 75-80: As Row 2.
Change to MC.
Rows 81-94: As Row 2.
Change to CC1.
Rep rows 15-94 once more. Fasten off, do not turn.

Border
Join MC to first st of last row.
Rnd 1 (RS): 1 ch (does not count as a st throughout border), 1 dc in each st and 1ch-sp to end of row, *rotate to work across row ends, 3 dc in first row end for corner, [1 dc in next row end] 172 times, 3 dc in last row end for corner**, rotate to work next edge, 240 dc across foundation ch, rep between * and **, join with sl st to beg dc. Do not turn. *836 sts*
Rnd 2: 1 ch, [dc across to next corner st, 3 dc in corner st] 4 times, dc to end, join with sl st to beg dc. *844 sts*
Change to CC1.
Rnds 3-4: As Rnd 2. *860 sts*
Change to MC.
Rnd 5: As Rnd 2. *868 sts*
Change to CC2.
Rnds 6-7: As Rnd 2. *884 sts*
Change to MC.
Rnd 8: As Rnd 2. *892 sts*
Change to CC3.
Rnds 9-10: As Rnd 2. *908 sts*

How to... work into a chain space

Identify the next chain space. You can see the 'V' of the stitch in the row below, but we're working into the gap next to it.

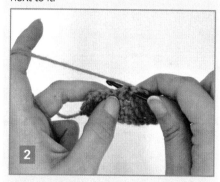

Insert hook into this space, pull up a loop so you have two loops on your hook.

Wrap the yarn around your hook and pull through both loops.

Chain one, which creates the chain space for your next row. Repeat steps 1-4 to end.

Fasten off. Weave in ends. 🧶

Special stitches

Puff (PS): [Insert hook into 3ch-sp, yrh, pul, drawing loop up to height of previous 3 ch, yrh] 4 times into the same 3ch-sp, draw through all 8 loops on hook
See page 26 for all other abbreviations

SHERBET PONCHO

This is a fun, quick and easy motif project for your special little person

🧶 4-ply 🧶 3mm

★ **Beginner friendly**

Yarn used

Cotton 4-ply
50g each in cream (A), bright blue (B), light orange (C), green (D) & pink (E)

Tension

Each granny square motif is approximately 13cm square

Hook used

3mm

Other supplies

- tapestry needle
- pompom maker

Sizing

One size: 9 months to 3 years

This colourful poncho is made in 6 motifs that are sewn together and then the edging is worked in rounds.

🔵 Start crocheting...

Squares

Make 6

Rnd 1: With A, chain 6 and join with a sl st to form a ring.

Rnd 2: 3 ch, 2 tr into ring, 2 ch, 3 tr into ring, [3 tr, 2 ch, 3 tr] 3 times into ring, join with sl st in top of beg 3-ch. Fasten off.

Rnd 3: Attach B to any corner 2-ch sp, 3 ch, [2 tr, 2 ch, 3 tr] into same ch-sp, [3 tr, 2 ch, 3 tr into next corner 2ch-sp] 3 times, join with sl st in top of beg 3-ch. Fasten off.

Rnd 4: Attach C to any corner 2ch-sp, 3 ch, [2 tr, ch 2, 3 tr] into same ch-sp, *3 tr into sp between 3-tr clusters on prev rnd, [3 tr, ch 2, 3 tr] into corner 2ch-sp; rep from * twice, 3 tr into sp between 3-tr clusters on prev rnd, join with sl st in top of beg 3-ch. Fasten off.

Rnd 5: Attach D to any corner 2ch-sp, 3 ch, [2 tr, 2 ch, 3 tr] into same ch-sp, *[3 tr into next sp] twice, [3 tr, 2 ch, 3 tr] into next corner 2ch-sp; rep from * twice, [3 tr into next sp] twice, join with sl st in top of beg 3-ch. Fasten off.

Rnd 6: Attach E to any corner 2ch-sp, 3 ch, [2 tr, 2 ch, 3 tr] into same ch-sp, *[3 tr into next sp] 3 times, [3 tr, 2 ch, 3 tr] into next corner 2ch-sp; rep from * twice, [3 tr into next sp] 3 times, join with sl st in top of beg 3-ch. Fasten off.

Rnd 7: Attach A to any corner 2ch-sp, 3 ch, [2 tr, 2 ch, 3 tr] into same ch-sp, *[3 tr into next sp] 4 times, [3 tr, 2 ch, 3 tr] into next corner 2ch-sp; rep from * twice, [3 tr into next sp] 4 times, join with sl st in top of beg 3-ch. Fasten off.

Rnd 8: Attach B to any corner 2ch-sp, 3 ch, [2 tr, 2 ch, 3 tr] into same ch-sp, *[3 tr into next sp] 5 times, [3 tr, 2 ch, 3 tr] into next corner 2ch-sp; rep from * twice, [3 tr into next sp] 5 times, join with sl st in top of beg 3-ch. Fasten off.

Rnd 9: Attach C to any corner 2ch-sp, 3 ch, [2 tr, 2 ch, 3 tr] into same ch-sp, *[3 tr into next sp] 6 times, [3 tr, 2 ch, 3 tr] into next corner 2ch-sp; rep from * twice, [3 tr into next sp] 6 times, join with sl st in top of beg 3-ch. Fasten off.

Schematic

13cm
26cm

Making up: Sew in all ends. Join 3 squares together to form the front and rem 3 squares together to form the back. Join front to back at shoulder seams.

Collar

Rnd 1: With poncho RS out, attach D to corner 2-ch space at top of middle square, dc into every st and 2ch-sp around the neckline, sl st into first st, fasten off. *107 sts*

Rnd 2: Attach E to any st, dc around, sl st into first st. Fasten off.

Lower Border

Rnd 1: Attach D to corner 2ch-sp at bottom of middle square, [dc, 2 ch, dc] into same sp, 103 dc, [dc, 2 ch, dc], 103 dc, sl st into first st, fasten off.

Rnd 2: Attach E to 2ch-sp corner at bottom of middle square, [dc, 2 ch, dc] into same sp, 105 dc, [dc, 2 ch, dc], 105 dc, sl st into first st, fasten off.

Rnd 3: Attach A to 2ch-sp corner at bottom of middle square, [dc, 2 ch, dc] into same sp, 2 dc, dc into 2ch-sp on Rnd 9 of square, [2 dc, dc into middle st of cluster on Rnd 8 of square] 7 times, *2 dc, dc into 2ch-sp on Rnd 9 of square, dc, dc into 2ch-sp on Rnd 9 of square, [2 dc, dc into middle st of cluster on Rnd 8 of square] 7 times**; rep from * twice, 2 dc, dc into 2ch-sp on Rnd 9 of square, 2 dc, [dc, 2 ch, dc] into ch-sp, 2 dc, dc into 2ch-sp on Rnd 9 of square, [2 dc, dc into middle st of cluster on Rnd 8 of square] 7 times; rep from * to ** twice, 2 dc, dc into 2ch-sp on Rnd 9 of square, 2 dc, sl st into first st, 1 ch.

Rnd 4: Dc, [dc, 2 ch, dc] into 2ch-sp, 109 dc, [dc, 2 ch, dc], 108 dc, sl st into first st. Fasten off.

Finishing

Weave in ends and attach pompoms. 🧶

Helio COWL

Sometimes simple is best – this granny cowl is perfect as a gift and can be whipped up in a weekend!

🧶 DK 🧵 3mm

★ Quick & easy

Yarn used

Acrylic DK
22g each in teal (A), light blue (B), white (C),
red (D) & yellow (E)

Tension

21 sts (7 blocks of 3) x 12 rows = 10cm

Hook used

3mm

Sizing

75cm circumference,
15cm depth

....

Crochet over the ends as you go, to save
time sewing in lots of ends at the finish

🌀 Start crocheting...

This pattern is worked in joined rounds,
join with a sl st in top of beg 3 ch, which
always counts as the first tr. Use a st
marker or waste yarn to keep track of the
first st of each rnd.

From Rnd 2, you will work into sp between
2 sets of 3 tr-blocks.

Change colour at the end of every rnd,
following the stripe sequence A, B, C, D, E.

With A, chain 159. Join to work in the rnd,
being careful not to twist.
Rnd 1: 3 ch (counts as first tr here and
throughout), 158 tr, join. Turn. *159 sts*

Rnd 2: With B, 3 ch, 2 tr in first st, miss 2
sts, [3 tr in next st, miss 2 sts] 52 times,
join. Turn. *53 3 tr-blocks*
Rnds 3-18: 3 ch, 2 tr in sp between 3tr-
blocks, [3 tr in next sp] 52 times, join.
Rnd 19: 3 ch, 1 tr in each st around.
Fasten off. Weave in ends.

Edging

Join E to end of Rnd 19, crab st around.
Fasten off. Rejoin E to bottom edge
and crab st around. Fasten off. Weave
in all ends. 🧶

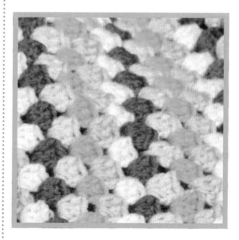

Techniques used

working in the round
changing colours
sl st
ch
tr
crab st: insert hook into next st to the
right, from front to back, yrh, pul, yrh,
draw through both loops on hook
See page 26 for all other abbreviations

Made in the USA
Middletown, DE
31 October 2024

63632574R00029